BARYSHNIKOV
ON BROADWAY

BARYSHNIKOV

PHOTOGRAPHS BY

FOREWORD BY WALTER TERRY

ON BROADWAY
MARTHA SWOPE

HARMONY BOOKS/NEW YORK

A special thank you to Susan Cook,
assistant to Martha Swope.

Book design by Ken Sansone
Editor: Harriet Bell

Scanned Alithotones and two-color black printing
by Alithochrome Corporation, Hauppauge, New York.

Printed in the United States of America

Published simultaneously in Canada by General Publishing Company Limited

Library of Congress Catalog Card Number: 80-81306
ISBN: 0-517-542188 (cloth)
0-517-542196 (paper)

10 9 8 7 6 5 4 3 2 1
First edition

FOREWORD

BY WALTER TERRY

"My God! Come here and look at this. I don't believe it!" The veteran American dancer-choreographer-director Ruth Page had just snapped on the TV as we came into her Chicago apartment from a ballet performance. There on the little black-and-white screen was a teen-age ballet dancer doing impossible things with his body. Page, who had danced with Diaghilev's historic Ballets Russes, performed with Pavlova, headed her own troupes, and introduced Rudolf Nureyev to America, was standing open-mouthed in front of the television set. "Who is it?" I asked. "They showed his name but I can't pronounce it, something like Barry . . ." The dancer was Mikhail Baryshnikov and this apparently amateur film clip had been made in Varna, Bulgaria, in the late 1960s when an unknown dancer from Leningrad's prestigious Kirov Ballet had won a gold medal at the famed International Ballet Competition.

Today, Baryshnikov belongs to America, almost everyone can pronounce his name, thousands have seen him dance the great ballet classics in theaters across the country, and millions have watched the world-famous premier danseur on television specials, but now, for the first time, vast audiences are able to see something they—and he—never dreamed would be possible: Baryshnikov on Broadway! There's another switch too. His partner here is not his fellow-countrywoman Natalia Makarova or the American Patricia McBride or any other prima ballerina but, rather, one of the great ladies of show biz, Liza Minnelli.

"Misha," as Baryshnikov is called by his friends (and the newspaper columnists!), told me in an early interview in halting English—it is fluent and wonderfully Americanese now—that "it is important for me to work in all styles possible. I should be able to dance anything assigned to me, anything I want to do. In this century a dancer should be a good technician, a good partner, a good actor, and he should be flexible in dancing in many, many styles."

At first, his thoughts were on modern ballets, even jazz-based ballets, unknown in Russia, and soon he was excelling in these as he long had done in Don Quixote, Giselle, and The Nutcracker (the latter in which he served as choreographer and star for national television). But he soon came to love Broadway and its artists, the great musicals unmatched anywhere else in the world, the music, and, especially, the dancing that offered in abundance those "many, many styles" that he hoped to conquer. With Liza Minnelli as his guide, as well as his singing, dancing, clowning partner, he has done just that in the super television extravaganza, "IBM Presents Baryshnikov on Broadway."

Squeals, gasps, gurgles, and roars emerge from the throats of his legion of fans when Baryshnikov on-stage glides, soars, spins, and woos defenseless heroines as the Prince Charming of many a ballet. Now those balletomanes, plus those millions who have never seen a ballet, can marvel at Misha as a cowboy, a low-down gambler, a Charleston cutup, a cancan dancer, a hot and sexy jazz dancer, a lithe companion to husky Nell Carter in "Honeysuckle Rose" and, especially, as Liza's newest Broadway partner in a television blockbuster written by Fred Ebb.

Liza Minnelli a dancer? Liza once said to the composer of many of her songs, John Kander, "My mother was a singer who danced. I'm a dancer who sings." And the daughter of Judy Garland and noted director Vincente Minnelli started out as a dancer. She attended New York City's celebrated vocational public school, the High School of Performing Arts, from whence came Arthur Mitchell, Edward Villella, Ben Vereen, and a host of other kids who went on to make it big in ballet, modern dance, jazz, movies, TV. Liza was a dance—not music or drama—major at this school. Sometimes after school hours the phone would ring and Judy Garland would ask Gertrude Shurr, Liza's modern dance teacher, "Do you know where Liza is?" The standard answer was "She's either at Luigi's watching a dance class or at Joffrey's watching a ballet class or rehearsal." Liza Minnelli has always been a dancer . . . who sings . . . and acts. Misha Baryshnikov has always been a dancer . . . who just now can sing and act.

There is a third star in this report on Baryshnikov on Broadway. She is a dancer too, although no one ever sees her dance. Her special gift is her ability to give eloquent permanence to fleeting moments of supreme beauty, to capture forever a moment of high passion or low-down humor, to record for posterity that instant of action that in performance is gone the very second it is born. Her name is Martha Swope, and her name on the cover of this book and everywhere else in the world of arts and entertainment is unmistakably star billing when it says "Photographs by Martha Swope."

There are many photographers who take great pictures. There are a few photographers in the world who take fine dance pictures. But there is only one Martha Swope. In my many years as a writer on dance and dancers, I have seen again and again that hopeful, expectant look on the faces of art directors of newspapers, magazines, books, souvenir programs, and even encyclopedias when I come in with a photo (or more) to illustrate something I have written. With that eager look goes, "I hope it's a Swope!" In publishing as in theater, "a Swope" means not only a picture that is clear and sharp and expertly composed, but also one that seeks out the heart of a scene, reveals the intent of a character and, in dance, zooms in on that breathtaking moment of action that has left both artist and audience breathless with excitement. It can be a leap or a laugh, a glissade or a glance, a split-jump or a side-splitting antic—Swope's got it.

"IBM Presents Baryshnikov on Broadway" is made possible by a grant to television by an industrial giant, International Business Machines; produced by Gary Smith and Dwight Hemion, with Herman Krawitz as executive producer, and with Mr. Hemion as director, it is being seen—and will be seen—by millions of TV viewers. But a television show, like a stage presentation, is the victim of the clock. When it is over, it's over. There is no chance to linger over a marvelous moment, to savor a special image. But here in this book we are invited to linger and to savor to our heart's pleasure.

Martha's camera has done something the TV camera did not do and that is to take us behind the scenes as Misha plays the piano, practices a song, learns a new step, and joins the chorus of A Chorus Line as Michael Bennett supervises the transporting of a lad who learned to dance on an ancient stage—where Nijinsky and Pavlova had appeared before him   to the hallowed boards of a hoofer's heaven, a Broadway theater. Martha takes us with her pictures on that magic journey that Misha embarks upon when the big practice mirror in his ballet studio turns into a "looking glass." And, like Alice of Wonder-land fame managed to do, he walks into a world he knows only in his dreams.

The plot of Baryshnikov on Broadway is the story of how this dream came true. Misha says quite simply, "There's no place like Broadway." Liza, bringing him a pastrami sandwich (with Russian dressing of course!) to his rehearsal, listens as he says, "I was thinking about A Chorus Line. That show gave the dancer dignity. It made the dancer a very important person," and Liza replies, "I think Chorus Line is a 'forever' show . . . like they have 'forever' ballets, Broadway has 'forever' musicals." Together they walk, or think, or believe their way through that mirror into what Liza describes as "some kind of Broadway wonderland" in an imagined song-and-dance panorama choreographed by Ron Field with a brand new number, "Showstoppers" by Kander and Ebb.

Many of the "forever" shows are in this TV wonderland and in this book of Misha by Martha. It never happened and it could never happen—not for real anyhow—that Mikhail Baryshnikov would dance "Once in Love with Amy," as Ray Bolger once did in Where's Charley?; or that he would join Liza for the "Shall We Dance?" number, an echo from The King and I; or don cowboy chaps and a ten-gallon hat for the braggart's recollections of high doin's in "Kansas City" from Oklahoma!; or find it "Too Darn Hot" (but not for Misha!) as wonderland takes him to Kiss Me Kate. And there is no question but that he's a knockout as a new member of the gang in A Chorus Line.

What a journey this has been for Misha in America: from a snippet of black-and-white film taken in Varna and seen in off-hours on a Chicago TV screen to an ABC-TV special, "IBM Presents Baryshnikov on Broadway," with lavish production, in glorious color, and on prime time. For Liza too, it is an important stop on a wonderful journey as she dances with one of the great male dancers of the century. And to see that this remarkable dual journey is not forgotten, who better than Martha Swope —the photo-favorite of both ballet and Broadway—to share with us her pictures of a magical journey to a modern wonderland.

Misha rehearses "Once in Love with Amy"
from <u>Where's Charley?</u> as choreographer
Ron Field looks on.

Assistant choreographers Marianne Selbert and
John Calvert teach Misha the "Cabaret" routine.

Misha rehearses "Once in Love with Amy"
as Ron Field looks on.

Misha and Liza Minnelli practice
"Too Darn Hot" from <u>Kiss Me Kate</u>.

Rehearsing the "Guys and Dolls" number.

Executive producer Herman Krawitz, producer and director Dwight Hemion, producer Gary Smith, and writer Fred Ebb watch a rehearsal.

Costume designer Theoni Aldredge goes over
the sketches with Misha (top).

John Calvert describes the set to Misha and
dancer Ravah Daley (bottom).

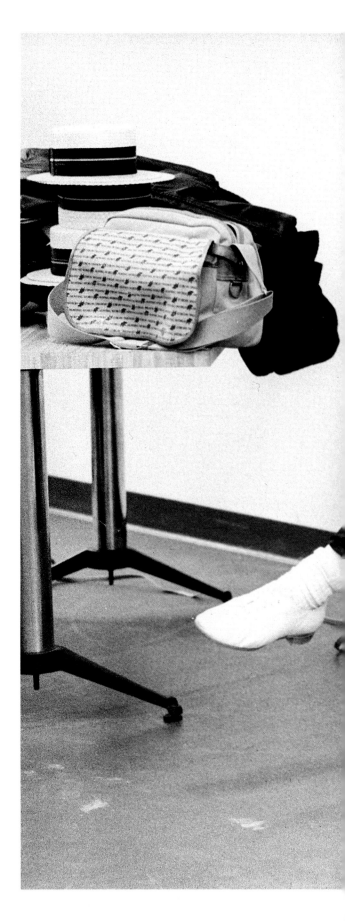

Recording session: Misha,
Fred Ebb, and Liza Minnelli.

Dress rehearsal for "Honeysuckle Rose:"
Misha and Nell Carter, star of Ain't Misbehavin'.

Misha, Dwight Hemion, and Gary Smith
(behind Misha) study the videotape (top).

The cast and choreographers present Misha
with a pair of tap shoes (bottom).

Misha as we know him (overleaf).

Liza guides Misha as he leaps into
the world of Broadway.

Misha's journey begins
with <u>Oklahoma!</u>

"Everything's Up to Date in Kansas City"

"Oklahoma!"

Liza introduces Misha
to <u>Ain't Misbehavin'</u>.

"Honeysuckle Rose"

Nell Carter and Misha.

Misha as Sky Masterson from <u>Guys and Dolls.</u>

42

Misha asks Liza, "Shall We Dance?"

Misha and Liza sing and dance Kander and Ebb's
"Showstoppers" production number.

"Won't You Charleston with Me?"

"Cabaret"

"Once in Love with Amy"

"Too Darn Hot"

CREDITS

"IBM Presents Baryshnikov on Broadway" starring Mikhail Baryshnikov and guest starring Nell Carter and the cast of A Chorus Line, with special guest star Liza Minnelli;

Theoni Aldredge, Costume Designer; Obba Babatunde, Dancer; Ralph Burns, Music Arranger; Billy Byers, Music Arranger; John Calvert, Assistant Choreographer; Don Correia, Dancer; Ravah Daley, Dancer; Lillian D'Honau, Dancer; Fred Ebb, Writer; Ron Field, Choreographer; Ian Fraser, Musical Director; Dorothy Freitag, Dance Arranger; Ed Greene, Audio; Dwight Hemion, Producer/Director; Don James, Dance Arranger; John Kander, Special Material; Herman Krawitz, Executive Producer; Charles Lisanby, Art Director; Barbara Matera, Costume Maker; Vera Mazzeo, Dancer; Gary Morgan, Dancer; Dennon Rawles, Dancer; Gerri Reddick, Dancer; John Rook, Lighting Director; Rita Scott, Associate Producer and Director; Marianne Selbert, Assistant Choreographer; Gary Smith, Producer; Connie Stone, Public Relations; Suzanne Walker, Dancer; Sammy Williams, Dancer.

A Chorus Line, through the courtesy of the New York Shakespeare Festival, Joseph Papp, Producer, in association with Plum Productions. Conceived, directed, and choreographed by Michael Bennett. Co-choreographed by Bob Avian. James Kirkwood, Nick Dante, Edward Kleban, and Marvin Hamlisch, authors of A Chorus Line.